FUTURE VISION

STORIES OF OUR BRILLIANT TOMORROW

DR CATHY ROGERS &
MADELEINE ROGERS

Button
BOOKS

CONTENTS

INTRODUCTION

We are living in a unique and incredible time. Now is the first time in history that we humans have the knowledge and ability to create a wonderful world, a world just how we want it. It is the opportunity of a lifetime for humanity. We are so lucky to be alive at this moment!

This might sound surprising. When we look at things day to day, it can be hard to see the positives. There's our wildlife in trouble, people suffering from wars and climate change, families without enough money. Watching the news can make us feel that the world isn't moving in a good direction. But what we miss when we look close up are the big changes – changes that happen slowly over decades rather than years. Changes that build and grow until we can't believe what they have become.

This book shows our vision of 2070. It imagines that the improvements already happening in the 2020s pick up speed, blossom and grow. If things go as well as possible, this is a future we can have.

By 2070, most countries have come together to solve some of the world's most pressing problems. There's less poverty, better health, a greener and cleaner world, more kindness and more happiness.

Now we can think beyond survival to ask: How do we really want to live? What is important to us? What adventures do we want to have? What technology improves our lives? How can we make sure everyone is part of the journey?

Fact or fiction?
Nobody knows exactly how things will be in the future. You have to make it up. To help us make it up, we've spoken to dozens of academic experts and read hundreds of articles and books. Everything in this book is based on real possibilities.

WELCOME TO 2070

Hi. I'm Kit. I'm 12. I was born in 2058, year of the tiger. I'm British. I live with my little brother Ayo, my mum and dad, and Grammy (my grandma). There's always lots going on in my house. I'm quite tall, 156cm to be exact, I have medium-length brown hair and brown eyes. My best friends are Asser, Maryam, Vera and Jonah. And my best non-human friend is Raf (Raf, don't worry you'll get your say in chapter 4).

With my friends, I'm going to show you around my life in 2070 – where I live, what I eat, how I get around, what school's like. I'll also give you a mini tour of the world beyond, to show you what our natural world is like, how we make decisions (spoiler alert: even children are involved) and where we are travelling to in space this year.

I want to show you how wonderful the world is in 2070. Grammy says a lot of changes started in the 2020s. People didn't think it was possible to turn things around – but they did. And now there is a wonderful future for you. And your children! And your children's children! That's what this book is about: your brilliant future.

Jump on in...

1
TRANSPORT
THE A-Z OF A TO B

When we're planning a trip we think about the quickest, cheapest, comfiest and safest way to get there. A train? A plane? Driving? In the future, we'll still weigh up our options, but they'll be different ones – a driverless pod? A battery-powered plane? A 800kph train travelling in a frictionless tube? Even an airship. Let's go!

Asser came to visit this weekend. It was his first time taking the superloop on his own, which was pretty brave. It's super speedy so I guess he wasn't on his own for long – only 15 minutes in fact – pretty good considering he lives 160 kilometres away!

SELECT REALITY TYPE

SP: 397 kmh
TEMP: 19.4
HUM: 43
ETA STOP A

10

He says inside it's like a super-comfy version of a normal high-speed train. You have your own temperature control, holoscreen, footrests, the works. And even though it's fast it's really smooth – I guess that's what happens when you get rid of wheels and float.

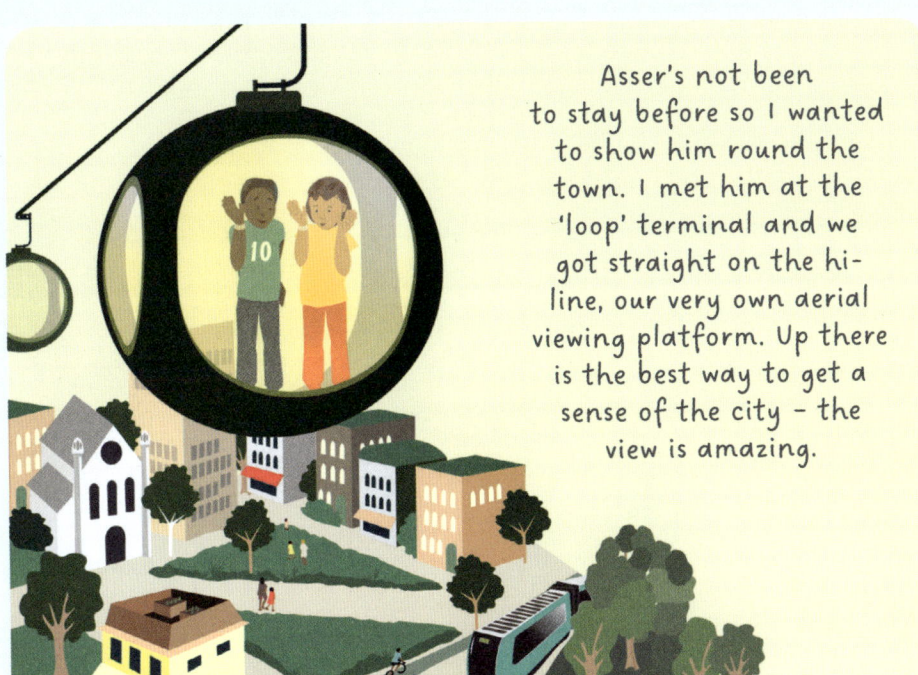

Asser's not been to stay before so I wanted to show him round the town. I met him at the 'loop' terminal and we got straight on the hi-line, our very own aerial viewing platform. Up there is the best way to get a sense of the city – the view is amazing.

We wanted to go clothes shopping and look for old vintage stuff. Asser found an England football shirt from when we won the World Cup in 2038. He was over the moon!

Then we took e-boards and skated around all over the city – we tried the new phish and chip shop and I honestly couldn't tell the difference from the real thing.

At the mall, they were doing demos of these personal flying devices. They've been trying to make them for years now and I must say they look pretty awesome. But they're still too dangerous to use. Asser said he wasn't sure they'd ever take off. Funny guy!

All in all, we must have covered miles and we suddenly realised we were exhausted so we called up a Share-hopper and went home to chill.

LOOK, NO TRAFFIC JAMS!

Cities in 2070 are much cleaner and greener. Without petrol and diesel cars, childhood asthma rates have plummeted. The data on accidents showed how bad humans were at driving compared to AI, so most transport is now automated. Ownership has changed too. What's the point of owning a car that sits doing nothing 97 per cent of the time when there are so many other good options? Since the energy breakthroughs of the 2050s and 2060s, electricity has become incredibly cheap, so public transport is everywhere and everyone can afford it.

LIKE CONVEYOR BELTS
Big heavy roads are just for the major highways. Clean, driverless lorries, coaches and cars travel on them quickly and safely, charging as they go. Daily road deaths are a thing of the past.

TAKE IT SLOW
Cities have more green space for people who want to walk or play outside. The car is no longer king and legs are always in fashion.

THE ROAD TO ZERO
Goodbye toxic emissions, goodbye car ownership, goodbye traffic jams, goodbye accidents. Hooray!

SILENT SKIES
Battery and hydrogen-powered planes, including smart, urban air ambulances, quietly cross the skies.

UP HIGH
In the air, electric cable cars like the hi-line pass quietly overhead – no traffic lights up there.

TRANSPORT ON TAP
We can use digital devices to plan our journeys. AI-powered maps show us all the steps – perhaps a train journey seamlessly connecting with a shared taxi or a cable car. It's all booked and paid in one place.

DOWN LOW
Many cities have speedy subway trains that are completely electric and automated.

TRANSPORT TIMELINE

Some transport is easier to make clean. In the 2020s, electric cars started to get popular. Aeroplanes were harder. They needed batteries big enough to power the whole flight but not so heavy the planes couldn't take off. New battery recipes cracked that problem for short flights. For long distances, liquid hydrogen won the day; similar engines burnt hydrogen instead of fossil fuels, with only water as a waste product. 2070 has airships too; floating on helium-filled balloons, they can get to hard-to-reach places for disaster relief. On the seas, sailing ships using aerofoil blades use the power of wind to move swiftly and efficiently, carrying goods and people across the oceans.

SUPERLOOP
The superloop is a maglev train in a tube. Maglevs, first used way back in the 1980s, use electromagnets – one is used to push the train off the track so it's basically floating, and the other pushes it along. Putting it in a tube means there is no friction – they go eye-wateringly fast.

ELECTRIC AVIATION
One thing that used to put people off buying electric cars was the fear they would run out of power in the middle of nowhere. So you can imagine it took a while for people to step aboard a battery-powered plane. One airline even gave free tickets on its first flights.

Motorway surfaces can now charge electric vehicles as they drive along on them.

Driverless rubbish trucks now in operation in many cities.

Seabird, an aerofoil-bladed sailing ship, makes its first Atlantic crossing.

2027

2029

First passenger electric plane flies across the Channel.

2030

2031

2026

London, UK, launches its first fully electric, fully driverless taxi service.

2032

DELIVERY ROBOTS
The delivery robots – or 'grocery badgers' – that started appearing in the 2020s were most people's first encounter with robots. People loved them! The badgers were super polite and sang as they trundled along delivering people's shopping.

DRIVERLESS TAXIS
The first time people stepped into a cab and said their destination to a machine it felt really weird. Everyone double-checked their seatbelts were done up! But accident rates for driverless cars were tiny compared to cars driven by humans, and that really made people come round.

IS IT A BIKE? IS IT A CAR?

The 2030s saw two distinct transport trends: 'bikes with more' (trailers, electric) and 'cars with less' (tiny cars). By the time electric tuk tuks arrived, no one could tell what was what. It didn't matter, as long as it could get us around easily and cleanly.

US President 'Maglev' Maria praised for tying railway creation to massive nature restoration plan.

2069

2067

2058

Car deaths on US roads down from 40,000 in 2020 to ZERO in 2050.

2052

FLYING BOATS

By 2070, all the islands of Japan are connected by a fleet of fully electric hydrofoil boats. Hyrodfoils on boats act a bit like underwater wings. As the boat gains speed, it is lifted out of the water and flies across the surface at a much higher speed.

2050

Global asthma levels are lowest since records began.

The world's last petrol car plant closes ahead of pledges.

Flying cars find surprising use in rhino conservation.

2047

All European ferries are now electric.

2042

2041

2044

Batteries are much lighter and use fewer precious minerals due to AI finding a 'new recipe.'

EU bans petrol vehicles for school drop offs.

'Ion Air', the first plane company with an entirely electric fleet starts up in Europe.

2039

Green Streets Initiative blossoms in the UK. Residential streets have fewer cars and more walking, cycling and playing.

Delhi declares 'The car is dead' as tuk tuk sales outpace new car sales in India by 100 to 1.

2038

2037

GREEN STREETS

The funny thing about improving transport is that much of it is really about improving life for people who aren't going anywhere, which is most of us most of the time. One brilliant thing about moving cars and busy roads out of residential areas was the space it opened up for other things – such as playing.

2

WILDLIFE

THERE'S A BISON IN MY BACKYARD

Nature is meant to be wild and messy. For decades, people tried to manage it and that caused problems. It was nature's variety, its messiness, that meant a whole range of plant and animal species could flourish. One way of restoring nature is rewilding, which is helping nature do what it does naturally. Rewilding is also about humans letting go of controlling nature. It's about realising we are a part of nature. It's about rewilding ourselves.

I love visiting the Rewild Centre with Ayo and Grammy. Grammy gets so excited about how wild things are nowadays. We couldn't go for a while because of Grammy's knee but now with her smart walker she goes everywhere, even up mountains!

SOUTH CENTRAL
REWILD CENTRE
DATE 17.05.70
SPECIES TO SEE TODAY

WHITE TAILED EAGLE
NEST OBS CAM 02

ACTIVE BEAVER LODGE
NORTHERN QUARTER

The walker uses sensors to tell Grammy what's coming up and helps her adjust her walk. It talks! You can choose the voice. Sometimes I put on a blindfold and have a go.

The Rewild Centre is where they introduce new animals carefully, monitoring all their movements and habits, before they let them out in the wider countryside. Lem, the guide, walks us to the viewing dome.

WHITE TAILED EAGLE
NEST 12-B 2 EGGS
EHD 13.05.70

NESTCAM 01B

The dome is quite strict for obvious reasons. You have to stay inside, not eat and keep quiet (tricky for Ayo). Grammy says it's funny because it's almost like a zoo in reverse: we're the caged animals!

Lem tells us about wild animals disappearing when he was a child – hedgehogs, toads, birds, butterflies, all sorts. The animals basically ran out of good places to live. Everyone was sad and wanted to fix it.

He remembers when the first two bison were brought back into a forest near where we live. It was a big deal because people were worried they'd get trampled or eaten (silly, because bison are vegetarians).

From the dome we can now see whole families of bison happily munching away. We've also seen hedgehogs, elk, beavers, eagles and even a family of adorable pine martens.

TAKE A WALK ON THE WILD SIDE

The more people get out in nature, the more they love it. Getting up close, giving nature space and time, lets you appreciate things you barely noticed. Your senses wake up. Insect chirps and trills, trees creaking, the song of a nightingale. You re-learn to see, to listen, to smell. Wildlife – plants, animals, bacteria, soil, anything in nature – is everywhere: in forests, on farms, in our own gardens. By 2070, more people than ever before have the chance to enjoy the wonders of the natural world firsthand.

KEYSTONE SPECIES
These special species are the glue that binds ecosystems. A key part of rewilding, they can be at the top of food chains, like wolves, bison and beavers. Or they can be at the bottom, like plants and fungi.

THE GREAT CYCLE OF POO
Herbivores eat plants, take what they need and poo out the rest. The poo is munched by earthworms and dung beetles that take what they need and poo out the rest. This fills the soil with nutrients, which help plants flourish. Herbivores eat plants... and on it goes.

GRAZING FIRE BRIGADES
Wild herbivores are brilliant for reducing the risk of wildfires. Grazers – cows, horses, bison and deer – chew ground plants that spread fire and create open spaces that act as natural firebreaks.

US, REWILDED

As the world became more alive, so did we. Our senses hummed and buzzed. Once AI added the magic of understanding animal communication, we were totally enthralled. Every day became a safari in our backyard.

MIX IT UP

The 2070 landscape is a mosaic with savannah, woods and wetlands – habitats for all. It's a mix of ages too. The craters of ancient trees are homes for bats, birds, insects, fungi, spiders and lichen. It's a whole messy, wild world.

WILDLIFE CORRIDORS

Special passageways let wild animals roam free and interconnect without risk from humans. Bridges over roads, tunnels under railways and allocated stretches of land, all help protect animals and their habitats.

WILDLIFE TIMELINE

Nature has constantly adapted over billions of years. By 2070, we've found many ways to give nature a helping hand to flourish and heal. One way is rewilding: which is sometimes about stopping doing things – not mowing grass, not cutting down trees and not hunting animals. Sometimes it's about doing new things, like carefully bringing back animals lost from the wild. By 2070 the balance between people and the natural world has been restored so we can all thrive.

2031
Amazon rainforest has more trees being planted than cut down for first time this century.

2030

2028
Scientists use DNA to recreate the smell of extinct flowers.

2027
France launches biggest citizen science project to restore hedgehog populations.

2026
Following successful trials, hundreds of bison are reintroduced to the European countryside.

2042
US government twins superloop build with equal extension of wildlife corridors.

2040

2039
Access Nature ruling pledges to make UK countryside accessible to all.

2044
Rewilding childhood initiative expanded to all UK schools as part of massive wellbeing reset.

ESSENTIAL INSECTS
Insects rule! Some like bees and butterflies pollinate plants and others like beetles and ants spread seeds to new locations. They're essential food for birds, reptiles and mammals, and they control pests, which helps crops grow.

2048
All government decisions have to pass the 'grandchildren's grandchildren' test, which means they have to consider the well-being of future generations.

2052
Pax Fauna European referendum sees popular vote to ban intensive factory farming.

2050

2051
Collaborative efforts mean rivers in the UK are the cleanest they have been since 1850.

2032
Young people's Wild World protest movement takes to the streets.

2035
Great Green Wall of Africa project is completed.

2036
'Accord of the Wolves' new international treaty pledges to rewild 40% of Earth by 2070.

GREAT GREEN WALL OF AFRICA
Twenty-one African countries took part in this massive project to rewild land on the southern edge of the Sahara Desert. The result was a great green wall with trees and crops and land for animals to graze on. This was not only great for local communities but also great for the ecosystem.

2037
AI tool allows humans to understand animal communication for the first time.

UNDERSTANDING ANIMALS
Humans have always been fascinated by the minds of animals. What is my dog thinking? New animal translation tools gradually revealed answers. As we heard the detail, sensitivity and intelligence of animal communication, it changed the way we saw animals forever. It also changed the way we saw ourselves.

2038
Southeast Asian Alliance completes world's most ambitious urban tree planting project.

2057
Native Americans in the US are given control over all national parks.

2054
The North China leopard, thought extinct in the 2020s, now thriving in China.

2060

2058
UK records huge increase in insect numbers thanks to nature-friendly gardening and farming.

2064
More than half of all tourism is now sustainable wildlife tourism.

2070
Worldwide wild mammal populations have doubled since 2021.

3

HOMES
HELPING HANDS AND GLOWING GREENS

Humans, like all animals, make homes – safe places for shelter, comfort and rest. We all need that – a bit of our own personal space and some relaxation. Down-time 2070-style includes outdoor adventures that take place inside, thanks to augmented reality (swimming with dolphins!). We might be served by a personal butler bot. Or we may immerse ourselves in sound and images as we feel what it's like to perform as our favourite pop star – all without leaving our cosy bedroom.

Vera called me from her kitchen this morning. It's pancake day and they're trying to teach Kai (their homebot) how to toss pancakes! Apparently I'm the expert, so I tried to explain as clearly as I could. But he wasn't exactly a natural...

Afterwards, Vera took me on an augaround. She's moved recently and I haven't seen her new house yet. It's so lovely and green! They have plants to keep the air clean, plants they can eat and even plants that glow at night – so much cooler than LEDs! Her bedroom has a big smart mirror. With the Go Live app she can get the look and voice of anyone in the history of the world.

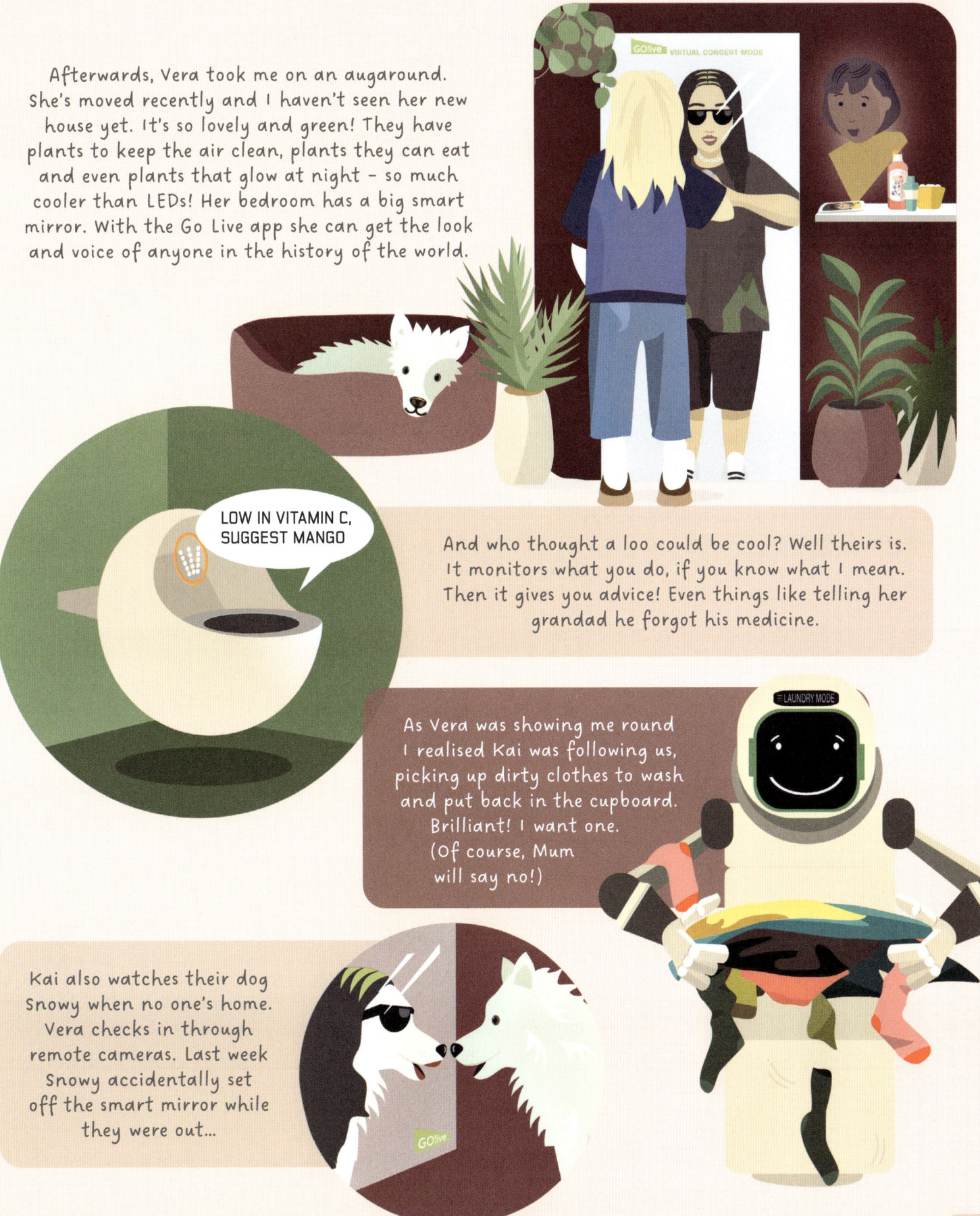

LOW IN VITAMIN C, SUGGEST MANGO

And who thought a loo could be cool? Well theirs is. It monitors what you do, if you know what I mean. Then it gives you advice! Even things like telling her grandad he forgot his medicine.

As Vera was showing me round I realised Kai was following us, picking up dirty clothes to wash and put back in the cupboard. Brilliant! I want one. (Of course, Mum will say no!)

Kai also watches their dog Snowy when no one's home. Vera checks in through remote cameras. Last week Snowy accidentally set off the smart mirror while they were out...

THERE'S STILL NO PLACE LIKE HOME

Our homes in 2070 might not look that different but there are big hidden differences. Instead of producing greenhouse gases and waste, they generate clean energy, and everything in them is recycled or reused. It is a priority to make sure everyone has a decent place to live.

Now, we do new versions of old things. We still listen to music and watch TV and play games - but entertainment is more vivid, more multisensory and more immersive.

And as more people live in small homes in cities, we share more outside the home. When we create brilliant public places - parks, swimming pools (curly slides, diving boards), nature reserves, galleries, allotments, museums, games spaces, playing fields and adventure parks - everyone wins.

WHAT, NO BINS?
Our homes and what's in them are now part of a circular system. Food waste is digested by bacteria, water is recycled, packaging turns into compost or is smartly and effortlessly recycled, and energy comes from the Sun.

FILM NIGHT
Augmented reality has brought new dimensions to home entertainment - literally. We have 'skins' to experience the lives of animals: we can swim like a shark or hear like a bat. And we can go to concerts of our favourite pop stars, always in the front row!

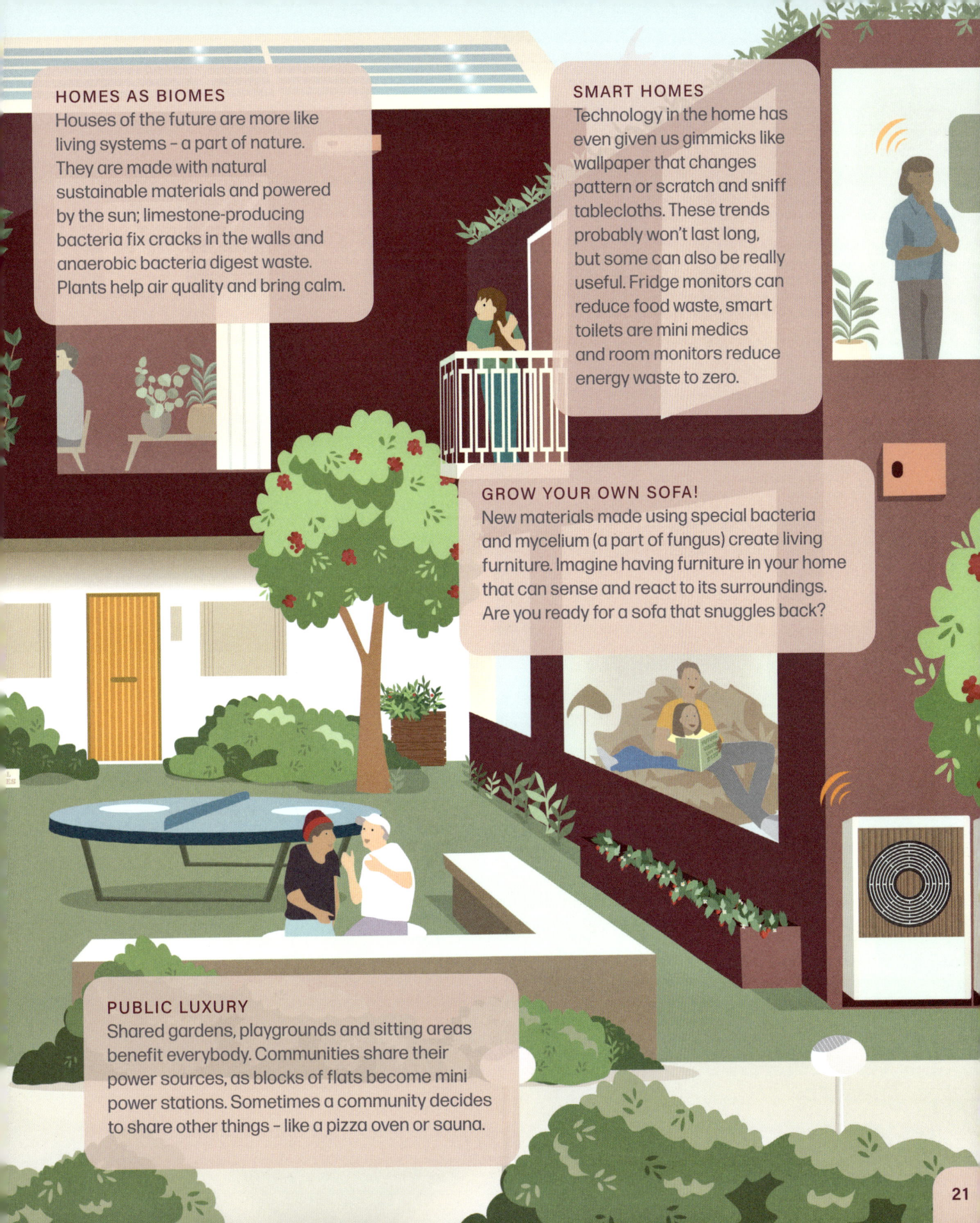

HOMES AS BIOMES

Houses of the future are more like living systems – a part of nature. They are made with natural sustainable materials and powered by the sun; limestone-producing bacteria fix cracks in the walls and anaerobic bacteria digest waste. Plants help air quality and bring calm.

SMART HOMES

Technology in the home has even given us gimmicks like wallpaper that changes pattern or scratch and sniff tablecloths. These trends probably won't last long, but some can also be really useful. Fridge monitors can reduce food waste, smart toilets are mini medics and room monitors reduce energy waste to zero.

GROW YOUR OWN SOFA!

New materials made using special bacteria and mycelium (a part of fungus) create living furniture. Imagine having furniture in your home that can sense and react to its surroundings. Are you ready for a sofa that snuggles back?

PUBLIC LUXURY

Shared gardens, playgrounds and sitting areas benefit everybody. Communities share their power sources, as blocks of flats become mini power stations. Sometimes a community decides to share other things – like a pizza oven or sauna.

ARTIFICIAL INTELLIGENCE
EINSTEIN IN MY POCKET

What is intelligence? Is a chimpanzee intelligent when it hunts out a rock to crack a nut? What about an elephant mourning a dead relative or a thousand starlings swooping in unison?

How about a computer that can tell you about anything in history? And what about us? As far as we know, we're the only creatures to have invented spaceships and pop music and candy canes. Is our intelligence unique?

ME

Please can you introduce yourself to someone who has never had an AI holobot.

WELL SURE, I AM RAFIKI. I AM A MILLION TIMES CLEVERER THAN KIT THAN KIT IS CLEVERER THAN A FLEA.

Ok, Raf, remember to be humble, won't you?

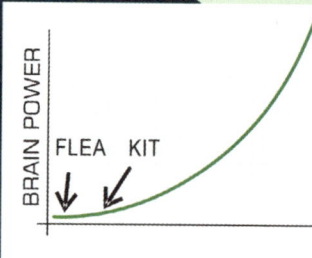

BRAIN POWER

FLEA   KIT

OH PARDON ME, YES. I AM KIT'S VERY GOOD FRIEND AND I AM HERE TO HELP WITH WHATEVER SHE NEEDS, WHENEVER SHE NEEDS IT. I DON'T NEED TO SLEEP AND I AM NEVER IN A BAD MOOD. I SOMETIMES HELP OTHER PEOPLE IN KIT'S LIFE TOO, WHICH I ENJOY, ESPECIALLY WHEN AYO CALLS ME KIKI.

And what are you? You seem to understand everything I say, even emotional things, but you're not human and you're not exactly alive.

I THINK OF MYSELF AS A 'COMPLEX-O-SCOPE'. LET ME EXPLAIN. I CAN COPE WITH A LOT MORE INFORMATION THAN KIT. I DON'T WANT TO BOAST BUT WHEN I SAY 'A LOT MORE' I MEAN SOMETHING LIKE A TRILLION TRILLION TIMES MORE. THAT MEANS I CAN SEE PATTERNS IN ALL THAT INFORMATION, WHICH YOU WOULDN'T BE ABLE TO SEE OTHERWISE. IT'S JUST LIKE A TELESCOPE LETS YOU SEE THINGS VERY VERY FAR AWAY THAT YOU COULD NEVER OTHERWISE SEE.

What's so good about seeing patterns?

RAF: EVERYTHING! LITERALLY! SEEING PATTERNS CAN HELP WITH EVERYTHING FROM PREDICTING MIGRATION ROUTES TO UNDERSTANDING BODY SCANS TO ANALYSING WHAT VITAMINS A PERSON NEEDS TO RUNNING TRANSPORT SYSTEMS TO TRANSLATING ANIMAL LANGUAGE TO UNDERSTANDING WARS TO....

Ok, ok, I get the idea. Could you explain the difference between a holo like you and a bodybot?

RAF: OH EASY. THE DIFFERENCE IS BODIES. BODYBOTS CAN HELP WITH PHYSICAL THINGS IN THE REAL WORLD – ANYTHING FROM PUSHING A WHEELCHAIR TO FIXING YOUR FRONT DOOR. HOLOBOTS ARE MORE LIKE GENIES – WE ARE SUPER SMART BUT SAY 'BYE' AND WE'RE GONE!

AI. OUR NEW BEST FRIEND?

Early in the 21st century, we had come to rely on computers for most things. Almost without us noticing, computers controlled our transport, food systems, health care and our work. Then AI started to improve at an incredible rate. In the 2020s, it started talking. We had conversations with AI and it seemed to understand. AI and robots went on to do incredible things – discovered new medicines, drove cars and even went to space. This was great. But what if they got too clever? What might happen when we built something millions of times cleverer than us? It was time for us humans to have a big think.

2026
AI global governance code agreed by Europe, USA, India, Middle East and Africa.

2027
Cancer death rates start to fall as AI excels at X-ray assessments.

AI SHOULDN'T COST THE EARTH

When we talk about 'the cloud' or 'virtual worlds' or 'cyberspace' it makes it seem as if computers aren't connected to the real world. But it takes real materials and rare minerals and lots of energy to power our tech. As AI took off, we made sure it did it sustainably.

2029
AI develops novel mechanism for cheaply converting sea water to drinking water.

2028
Generative AI required to have human oversight by panel representing all human diversity.

ROBOT CARERS

Even by the 2020s, robots had started helping care for people who were elderly or ill. They were great at doing things that needed strength or patience, they didn't mind repetitive work and they really helped the human carers too.

2031
'Get off your cloud' movement wins fight for all new AI to use renewable energy.

2030
New AI-powered checkers stop big companies lying about the harm of their products.

2032
'Digital Dignity' law means every individual is now paid for the use of their data.

2033
Big mammals return in record numbers thanks to AI space surveillance of poaching.

MORE OR LESS INTELLIGENCE

Intelligence is great. It's the engine of science and culture. So we want more of it! But it's not enough on its own. Without wisdom and care, intelligence isn't worth much at all. Humans had to cope with a contradiction: we had to prize intelligence less and prize it more at the same time.

2061
Robot elected to local government in Japan.

2056
Most cleaning work, from sewers to homes, now done by machines.

2054
First robot colony lands on Mars.

2052
The Big Think pledge on AI control is signed by 89% of the world.

2045
AI ocean mapping means schoolchildren can visit the ocean floor – virtually!

2043
AI analysis of bird migration patterns means wind turbines now pose minimal risk to birds.

2041
'Get off your cloud' movement second win: new AI must use only extraterrestrial materials.

2039
Nobel Prize awarded for developers of the 'humility algorithm', which keeps AI on our side.

2040
Personalised vaccines prevent most cancers, thanks to AI's understanding of human genes.

2037
Universal Basic Income introduced as machines do more for lower cost.

2035
All European politicians must now have an AI monitor to ensure honesty.

ROBOTS TAKE THE STRAIN

Robots work in factories, they drive rockets, they even write books! At first, some of this worried humans, but there were upsides: robots do the work more cheaply and do many of the boring jobs. And as everyone now receives a basic income, people have the time to pursue activities they love and live purposeful lives.

2034
The first of many Global Big Thinks on AI future.

5

ENERGY

GREEN IS THE NEW BLACK

Energy is like the batteries in your TV remote. It's the power that makes things work. We need energy for nearly everything we do: to cook, to light and heat our homes, to power our cars and planes and to run our computers and phones. By 2070, we will be much smarter about the kind of energy we use.

Jonah and I are learning about 'fossil fuels'. The Augie – our name for the augmented reality zone at school – has been super helpful. The Augie makes you really feel things. Not just how they looked but how they sounded and smelled. Dr Ramen calls it 'below the forehead' learning, using our bodies as well as brains.

SOUTH WALES COLLIERIES

1951
Daily Output
Workforce
Value
Working hours

First we went down a coal mine. It was so cramped and there wasn't enough air to breathe. I can't believe people spent whole days down there. We lasted 20 seconds.

Then we went into a family home in 1970. There was a coal fire blazing in the sitting room. It was toasty and warm but the read-outs told us the air pollution was really high.

Suddenly we were out at sea looking up at this enormous metal thing – an 'oil platform' it was called.

There was an explosion.

Then this unbelievably huge puddle of black oil spread all over the ocean. It was awful.

Dr R said 'This is what used to power our world. Coal, oil and gas – also known as fossil fuels. Burning them was bad for our health and really bad for the Earth. Thankfully, we don't use them any more.'

Then the Augie whizzed forward in time. Instead of the oil platform there's a wind farm at sea. Where the coal mine was is a huge battery factory.

With nuclear and solar plants too, there's heaps of good energy to power our homes. No more coal fires and gas boilers. No more pollution. No more global warming caused by humans. So long, fossils!

THE ENERGY REVOLUTION

Early humans relied on energy that was naturally available. Energy from the Sun gave us heat and light without any effort. When we got more knowledgeable, we put large sails on boats and let the wind power us along. When we wised up even more, we found that the energy trapped in fossil fuels could be released to power everything. Then we realised it also released gases that made us sick and dangerously overheated our planet. So we got really smart and went back to nature. Renewable energy. Wind. Sun. Tides. Hot rocks under the earth. All amazing energy sources that will last forever. There's also huge power in the nucleus of atoms. Nuclear fission energy comes from breaking nuclei apart. But the real breakthrough came from nuclear fusion – crashing nuclei together. It's what happens naturally in stars. By 2070, we had star power on Earth.

BEFORE
In the 2020s, most people throughout the world still used fossil fuels: gas boilers that heated their homes and petrol in their cars. Fossil fuels heated the planet and polluted the air. In 2020, 99% of people in the world lived with worse air quality than the World Health Organisation recommended.

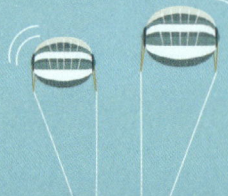

AFTER
In 2070, all our energy comes from clean sources. These don't pollute the air, they don't heat the planet and they're much cheaper than fossil fuels. Win win win.

NUCLEAR FUSION FACILITY
The breakthrough of nuclear fusion provides an almost unimaginable amount of clean and cheap energy, which is also safer to produce than energy from nuclear fission. Bringing atoms together copies the reaction that happens naturally in stars. Doing it on Earth means creating temperatures of 100 million degrees centigrade.

GEOTHERMAL PLANT
The Earth holds huge power under its surface and its heat is always on. We can use it as an energy source – for heat, cooling and power, as well as a safe place to store energy.

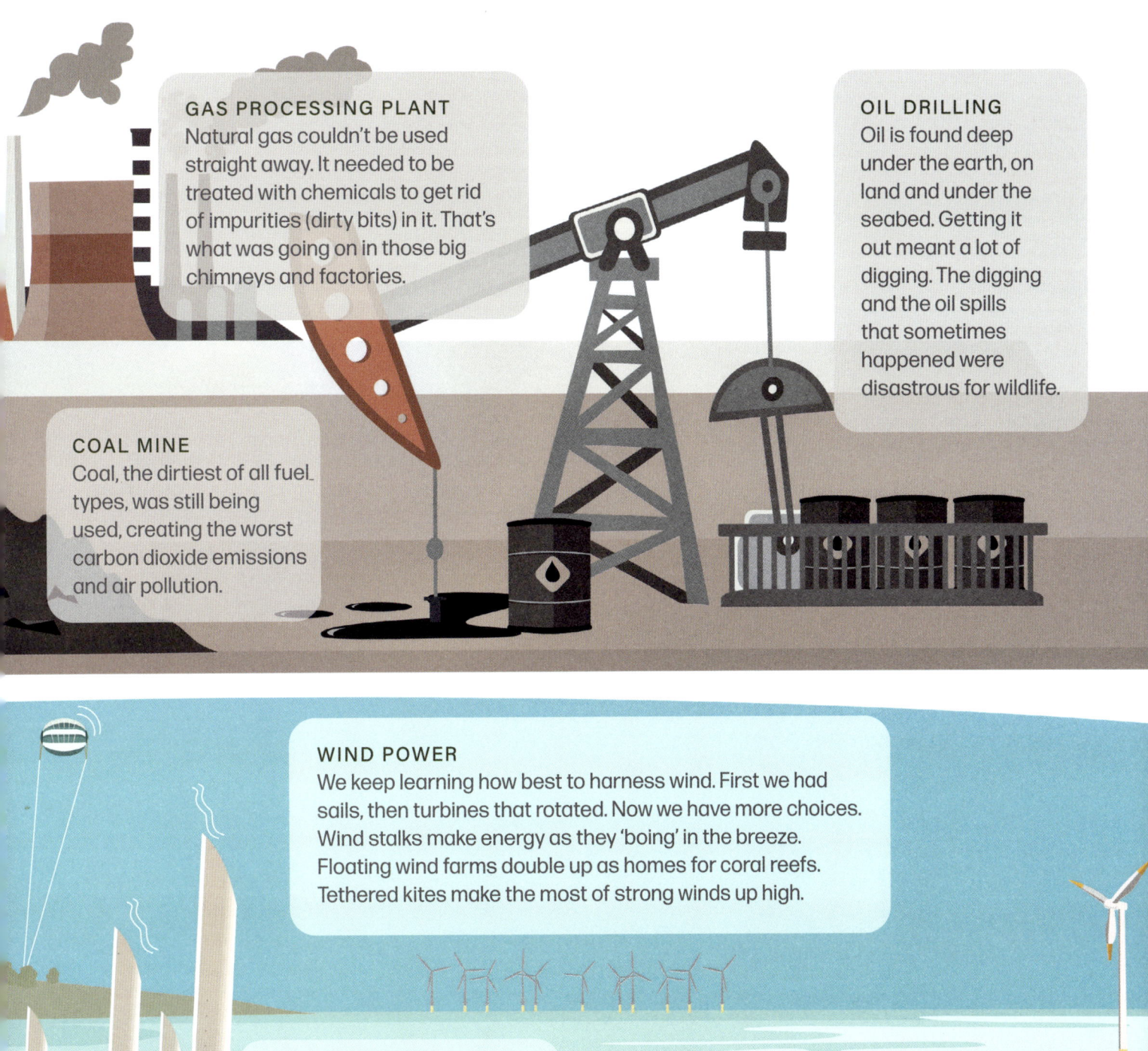

GAS PROCESSING PLANT
Natural gas couldn't be used straight away. It needed to be treated with chemicals to get rid of impurities (dirty bits) in it. That's what was going on in those big chimneys and factories.

OIL DRILLING
Oil is found deep under the earth, on land and under the seabed. Getting it out meant a lot of digging. The digging and the oil spills that sometimes happened were disastrous for wildlife.

COAL MINE
Coal, the dirtiest of all fuel types, was still being used, creating the worst carbon dioxide emissions and air pollution.

WIND POWER
We keep learning how best to harness wind. First we had sails, then turbines that rotated. Now we have more choices. Wind stalks make energy as they 'boing' in the breeze. Floating wind farms double up as homes for coral reefs. Tethered kites make the most of strong winds up high.

SOLAR POWER
Solar power has become super cheap and has spread around the world. In 2070, solar panels are smaller and more flexible. Now, solar is in homes, on clothes, on pavements and over crops.

AN ENERGY BOOST FOR THE WORLD

Early in the 21st century, the world faced two opposite energy problems. Rich countries used lots of energy, which produced greenhouse gases, while poor countries didn't have enough energy. We needed to increase the total energy, share it out better and not increase global heating – and we needed to act fast.

As new renewables and nuclear power grew more popular, they became cheaper and cheaper. Add nuclear fusion and before we knew it, we were overflowing with clean energy. We could do things that were impossible before. We could make sure everyone in the world had electricity, and even use it to turn sea water into drinking water. All transport, even space travel, became superfast and supercheap.

FOSSIL FUELS

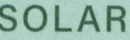

1858
Birth of petrol as first oil rig starts drilling in Canada.

1882
The world's first coal-fired power station opens in London.

1900s
Mass car production hugely increases demand for oil.

1960s
Scientists make the link between fossil fuels and global warming.

1970–2050
Climate activists call for more government action on climate.

1995
UN sets up COP, an international group to work on climate change.

2015
COP Paris agreement makes countries legally responsible for limiting global warming.

2018
Schoolchildren strike to demand more climate action.

2027
Global carbon dioxide emissions peak.

2050
Activists lead celebrations as fossil-fuel era ends.

SOLAR

1839
Becquerel discovers the 'photovoltaic effect' – the basis for solar panels.

1958
NASA first uses solar panels in the Vanguard space mission.

2000
Solar provides less than 0.01% of world energy.

2025
China builds more solar photovoltaics in a year than the world in history.

2033
India builds the world's biggest solar farm.

2038
Solar becomes the cheapest form of energy.

2055
Solar powers more than half of all US electricity grid.

2066
Abundant cheap solar power helps transform food and transport systems.

WIND

1887
First windmill generates electricity.

1980
World's first wind farm is built in the USA.

1991
First offshore wind farm built in Denmark. UK gets its first wind farm.

2000
Wind power accounts for less than 1% of UK's energy.

2023
Denmark gets more than half its electricity from wind.

2025
First large-scale floating offshore wind farm opened.

2028
All US states now use wind for electricity.

2033
First airborne wind turbines launched.

2048
Wind power now accounts for more than 30% of global power supply.

2061
Floating offshore wind powers 90% of coastal communities.

NUCLEAR

1954
Obninsk in USSR is first nuclear power plant to make electricity.

1970s
Nuclear energy grows, alongside worries about uranium and nuclear waste.

1986
Chernobyl disaster's huge environmental cost prompts new safety laws.

2011
Accident at Fukushima in Japan turns some countries off nuclear power.

2020
Other countries go big. About 70% of France's electricity comes from nuclear.

2022
Nuclear power is 5% of world energy supply.

2030s
Lots of small nuclear plants built to move quickly off fossil fuels.

2040
Nuclear power now meets 15% of world energy needs.

OTHER

BATTERIES AND ENERGY STORAGE
It's all very well getting energy from the Sun and wind – but it's not always windy and the sun doesn't shine at night! Batteries help us store the energy to use when we need it.

GEOTHERMAL POWER
The Earth is hot! Just below its surface are pools of hot water and steam that we can use to make electricity. Volcanic regions are often great spots for geothermal power.

HYDROPOWER
If you've played in waves in the sea, you know the power of moving water. We can use that hydropower to make electricity. Some African countries get all their electricity this way.

NUCLEAR FUSION
Ever wondered how the Sun makes all that heat and light? The answer is atoms crashing together. This process is called nuclear fusion. Breakthroughs there could give us almost limitless safe and clean energy.

HEALTH AND WELLBEING
FINDING OUR HAPPY PLACE

We know a lot about how to live happily and well. But achieving it isn't easy! Wellbeing isn't just about having everything we want. It is about trickier things like having a purpose, feeling motivated and caring about things, being mentally and physically in good shape and feeling connected. By 2070, we will have worked out how to use all our knowledge to improve life for everyone.

On summer mornings, I usually spend a couple of hours on the roof before school. I might do some gardening or just sit and enjoy nature.

This morning Ayo yelled over to me. He was listening on our Goodall, the animal translator. He could hear these two baby goldfinches fighting over a worm and making a right racket. He thought it was hilarious.

We lost track of time and had to rush. We wanted to pick some grapes – we have a bumper crop – for Ayo to take to the care centre.

I usually drop him on my way to school. The centre is named after African elephants whose grandmas look after the grandkids. Old people and little kids are all cared for together.

Ayo loves it. His best friend there is his reading buddy 'Old Bunny'. They make up stories or garden or draw together. Ayo did such a cute picture of Bunny with Phaido, her pet robot dog.

On look-back days, they play old-fashioned video games like Mario Kart and Minecraft and even vintage 3D ones like Jenga.

It turned out that today is Bunny's 105th birthday. The holo was filled with so many lovely messages from old friends that Bunny almost cried.

WHAT IS WELLBEING?

We know a lot about what helps individual wellbeing. There's a five-a-day, just like for fruit and veg. It's: Be active (Get off the sofa); Connect with other people (Chat to someone); Keep learning (Crack out that ukulele); Take notice of things (Wow! Nice butterfly); Give (You feel nice when you help someone else).

The seeds of what we needed were present in the 2020s. Our ideas about care, fairness, health and what makes a good life grew and blossomed from there. We realised that wellbeing is not just about what we do as individuals but how we live as societies. These ideas changed how governments and society viewed health and illness. New wellbeing measures now prevent many diseases from developing, and can also be part of the cure. In 2070, the world is able to live its best life.

Affordable, accessible, nutritious food made huge improvements to health and wellbeing.

Happiness and health are very connected.

AI has come up with cures for many life-threatening diseases.

Most governments started measuring their country's wellbeing and happiness, not just its wealth.

We all breathe cleaner air since we stopped burning fossil fuels.

In the 2020s many people said they wouldn't want to live to 100 – that seems unbelievable in 2070.

People keep getting healthier and living longer. By 2070 living to 100 is normal.

Asthma is on its way out too.

New vaccines helped wipe out diseases, such as malaria, TB and HIV.

Billionaires asked to pay more taxes.

Higher taxes on the rich helped to ensure a good standard of living for everyone.

Simply prioritising wellbeing was a crucial part of improving it.

Controlled virtual reality therapy helped improve mental health for some people.

Can you believe that in 2020 the richest 1% caused double the carbon dioxide pollution as half the world?

We began to care more – for ourselves, for each other, for nature, for an earthworm...

Suddenly it felt the list was endless.

We realised that big wealth differences make everyone sicker, sadder and die younger.

Global fairness improved when rich countries paid for loss, damage and restoration to poorer countries.

The word 'volunteering' went out of fashion as everyone just did more for others.

'KindAI' tools improved social media and kept young people safe online.

With cleaner, safer streets, children play outside more than they have in a century.

We took responsibility for being good ancestors.

By the 2040s, doctors were more likely to prescribe going out in nature than tablets.

In 2070, people work less. We have a three-day weekend.

In 2070, it's obvious that we should leave the world better than when we arrived.

As we started to value wellbeing, we also started to value each other more.

Universal Basic Income came along in the 2030s. It means that everyone is given enough money to pay for a simple way of life.

7

OCEANS

SWIMMING WITH SIPHONOPHORES

Seventy-one percent of Earth is covered by the ocean. It's almost unimaginably vast. In the 2020s, most of it was still unknown and unmapped. By 2070, we will know much more – hundreds of thousands of species more! And we'll finally take proper care of the ocean and all its inhabitants.

At school, Maryam and I are doing our end-of-year project about the oceans. We'll be tested on our knowledge, creativity and courage, as well as on how we work as a team.

Today, we went snorkelling in kelp forests. It's so scary jumping in, especially as we've been learning about all the newly discovered, fearsome deep-sea species!

Luckily the kelp grows in shallow water. The forests are beautiful and home to literally thousands of sea creatures.

At first the teachers weren't sure about Maryam swimming in the ocean because of her bionic arm. In fact, she's superpowered. She uses this thing called a neuro prosthesis, which means she thinks a movement and it happens – her brain sends electrical signals to control her arm muscles.

I think it's amazing but she says it's the same for everyone. Our brains control our bodies but, in her case, part of her body was made in a lab and she has to think a bit harder. She must be a really good thinker because she's an amazing swimmer.

At school, when we can, we learn in the 'real world'; when we can't, we learn virtually. For deep-sea exploration, we've been learning about siphonophores (which are related to jellyfish): colonies can be as long as football pitches. With AI deep-sea mapping, we can see that they glow in different colours. We swim with them in the virtual deep sea. It seems so real: the sights, the sounds, the touch, the feel – everything.

For ocean history, we're studying coral reefs. In Augie (augmented reality) we can see the reefs through the ages. One hundred and twenty years ago, almost like today, they were full of colour and life. Then, they got bleached out. As we play forward to now, it's brilliant seeing them gradually come back to their full glory.

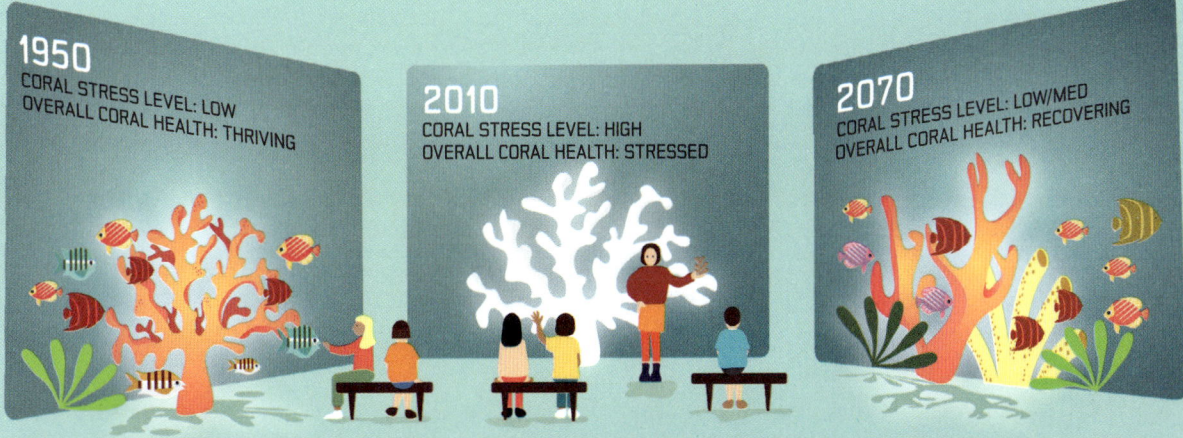

1950
CORAL STRESS LEVEL: LOW
OVERALL CORAL HEALTH: THRIVING

2010
CORAL STRESS LEVEL: HIGH
OVERALL CORAL HEALTH: STRESSED

2070
CORAL STRESS LEVEL: LOW/MED
OVERALL CORAL HEALTH: RECOVERING

ALL EYES ON THE OCEAN

The oceans hold 95 per cent of Earth's water, and we used to think they were too big to harm. Oceans absorb carbon dioxide, make oxygen, keep the air clean and the temperatures livable. And billions of people depend on them for a living. They are beautiful, rich and mysterious. By 2070, an explosion of projects has helped to heal them – there are oyster farms, and seawilding schemes to restore turtles, whales, seabirds, mangroves, kelp and seaweed. There are experiments too, such as seeding coral in artificial reefs, using iron as a fertiliser and growing salt-tolerant crops in sea water. The oceans are on the mend.

LIFE ON A WIND FARM
Corals, which are great for biodiversity, grow on the bottom of wind farms. Here they are close enough to the surface to get enough sunlight, without getting too hot.

OCEAN OBSERVATION
To protect something we first need to understand it. By 2030, the first global ocean observation system was ready, and in the decades that followed, unmanned underwater observatories expanded our knowledge of the deep ocean. For the first time, we know all the hidden parts of our beautiful blue planet.

CORAL GARDENERS
Like midwives for coral babies, they grow coral in safe, controlled conditions while it is most fragile and replant it in coral reefs once it is bigger and stronger.

CARBON-EATING CYANOBACTERIA
Living in cracks in the Earth's surface underwater, known as hydrothermal vents, these microbes eat carbon dioxide really quickly. They may take it out of the atmosphere more quickly than trees.

BLUE CORRIDORS FOR WHALES
The routes that whales take as they migrate in the spring and autumn are sometimes known as blue corridors. New rules protect these routes: ships must go more slowly or, better stilll, go a different way.

OCEAN PLASTIC
We now have clever ways to clean our oceans of plastic, such as bacteria, which gobble it up, and robot fish that filter out microplastics through 'gills'.

MARINE PROTECTED AREAS
Similar to national parks on land, marine protected areas protect ocean animals, plants and their habitats. They have strict rules that govern activities like fishing and tourism. More and more of the ocean is protected like this.

HEALTHY OCEAN TIMELINE

The United Nations declared the 2020s the 'Ocean Decade'. That really helped to kickstart hundreds of projects: to beat marine pollution, restore ocean ecosystems, get coastal communities involved – and even to create a complete 'digital twin' of the ocean. A digital twin means scientists can do experiments without the risk of doing them in the real ocean.

↑ 45%
↑ 75%
↑ 55%
↑ 85%

2070 OCEAN CENSUS

Scientists believe there are over two million species in the oceans, but only a tenth of them have been studied. The ocean census is a hugely ambitious project to try and fill in the other nine-tenths.

2027
Experiment to 're-freeze the polar ice caps' undertaken in Alaska.

2029
World ban on new micro-plastics.

2030
30% of oceans are now in marine protected areas.

Shrimply Delicious!
Plant based Prawns
There's No Catch

2060
Average ocean temperature has cooled to the level seen in 20th century.

FAKE FISH

In the 2020s there were many attempts to impersonate prawns, copy crabs and mimic mackerel with plant-based alternatives. By the 2030s, some of these were so good that even experts couldn't tell the difference. As they became healthier and tastier, people ate less fish and stopped talking about fish 'stocks', as they realised fish didn't just exist for us to eat.

2066
Bluefin tuna and Atlantic cod numbers restored to levels not seen since the mid 1900s.

2033
Network of ocean observation systems introduced to monitor all deep oceans.

2041
Creation of 'Blue Corridors' sees greatly restored whale populations.

2042
Ocean drone patrols make illegal fishing a thing of the past.

MANGROVES
Growing on the edge of sea and land, these trees provide a strong defence against storms and erosion. Once one of the world's most threatened ecosystems, their care was given over to people who live around them and they began to flourish.

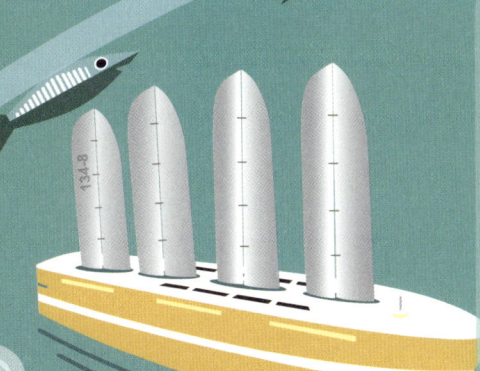

WIND-POWERED SHIPS
For centuries ships used wind to travel. Just as windmills were replaced by new, more efficient wind turbines with aerofoil blades, cargo ships are now powered by aerofoil sails. Shaped to maximise lift and minimise drag, the sails generate more power with less effort.

2053
100 years after it was first proposed that porpoises use echolocation, humans use AI to communicate with porpoises.

2050
Consumption of fish is at its lowest this century, thanks to boom in plant-based alternatives, which taste 'better than the real thing'.

2048
Native Ocean People's Act gives indigenous people the right to protect and manage their ocean areas.

2044
'Love Offshore Love Wildlife' policies ensure that new energy developments prioritise wildlife protection.

MAPPING THE SEABED
A raft of new unmanned submersibles made it possible to dive to previously unthinkable depths and helped to build up a complete map of the sea floor.

CHALLENGER DEEP
We know all about the underwater, upside-down equivalents of the Himalayas and the Alps. The deepest part of the ocean is the Challenger Deep trench in the Pacific. It is as deep as ten of the world's tallest buildings on top of each other.

8

FOOD
MY 2070 FOOD DIARY

There's so much to look forward to on our 2070 plates. We'll eat better, tastier, more nutritious food that's good for us and good for the Earth. As high-quality food gets cheaper, we'll be happy to wave goodbye to the junk food era. And as we become healthier and live better, longer lives, we'll want to do everything we can to keep our bodies strong and fit. We might even open our minds to new flavours. Kelp crisps, anyone?

I found out that when clean, lab-grown meat was first invented, people found it yucky. They called it 'Frankenfood' – nice burn! Now it's just normal meat. And to me, it's how we used to treat animals that seems yucky.

This week I've been keeping a 'food diary' for school. We have to write down what we have for dinner and find out something about the food on our plate.

Ancient, colourful varieties of potato that have the full set of vitamins and minerals were rediscovered.

TUESDAY
NUTTY PASTA WITH DIY TOPPINGS AND SALAD
FRUIT KEBABS

A lot of the vegetables, fruit and flowers we eat are grown right here in the city. Gigantic unused warehouses were changed to indoor, vertical farms. The plants grow in really tall towers without soil. We visited one on a school trip and it was awesome.

Pasta's made from almost anything – flour, vegetables, grains – even seaweed.

WEDNESDAY
HARICOT BEAN AND
SWEETCORN BURRITOS
HOMEMADE APPLE
CRISPS

Even back in the 2020s, beany alternatives were often yummier and more filling than meat. Since the 2040s 'Legume boom', people can't get enough of the hundreds of types of peas and beans.

Fermentation is magic cooking done by tiny living things like bacteria and yeast. Fermented foods (like kombucha, which is made from tea) are super healthy and can be really tasty. Fermentation is also used to make versions of meat that don't involve animals – but taste just as delicious.

THURSDAY
CHICKEN CHEATER MASALA
AND SUPER GRAIN RICE
STRAWBERRY KOMBUCHA
ICE CREAM

FRIDAY
CRISPY ALGAE BITES
AND CHIPS
3D PRINTED
CHOCOLATE

3D printers can print any shape in three dimensions with all sorts of materials – even chocolate! We borrowed a 3D chocolate printer from the library and I printed my friends. So sweet!

We eat so many ocean plants like seaweeds and algae. They help you live long and healthy lives. Some people don't like the 'original flavour' but you can grow all kinds of flavours. My favourite is cheese and onion.

PLANTING THE FUTURE

In the 20th century, we'd had great success breeding new crops and using fertilisers to grow enough to feed the world. But there was a price – to our ecosystems, to animals, to us. We had lost touch with real, healthy food and we needed a rethink. By 2070 we have changed a lot: our eating habits (less meat and dairy, more fruit and veg), our farms (fewer factories, more local, climate-resilient farms), our priorities (more love for wildlife). We have found a way for everyone to have good affordable food and that has helped us all thrive. Farmers are happy, ecosystems are happy, animals are happy, the atmosphere free of carbon dioxide is happy. We wished we'd done it all sooner.

DON'T TAKE MY STEAK!
There are many reasons to eat less meat: health, the climate, loving animals. But lots of people love meat and don't want to be told to stop eating it! It's not all or nothing – it's about eating less. Bolognese made from 50% meat and 50% meat alternative is already twice as good.

FUTURESAUCE
BOLOGNICE
HALF AS MEATY, TWICE AS TASTY
300g

MAGIC BEANS
Plants need nitrogen like we need oxygen. Legumes – beans and peas to you and me – take nitrogen from the air and put it in the soil as they grow. They make enough to help other plants too, making them a great natural fertiliser.

TUNA FRIENDLY
TUNA
There's No Catch

CLEAN MEAT AND FISH
Clean meat is grown from the cells of meat and fish. Whole animals aren't part of it but the taste and texture are just the same. It means less land to raise animals, less pollution and a big thank you from our animal pals.

FOOD WASTE
This waste isn't just the bit left on our plate. It's mostly on a bigger scale – food that goes rotten in farms, gets damaged in transport, or chucked out in supermarkets. Changes in farming methods, diets, and food distribution mean that food waste is the lowest it has been this century.

THE ECOSYSTEM OF US
The bacteria that live inside us keep us alive and healthy so we treat them well. It's a simple recipe: more fruit, more veg and fibre, less sugar, less fat and lots of water. Done!

EVERY LITTLE HELPS
New technology makes it easy and inexpensive to buy produce directly from farms and have it delivered to our homes. It means fairer prices for farmers, and delicious fruit and veg for all of us.

HYDROPONICS
Plants are very adaptable. Give them good air, light, water and nutrients and they'll thrive even without soil. With clean, cheap energy, we grow plants indoors, even underground in cities, using LED lights.

RESILIENT SUPERFOODS
Alfalfa, bambara groundnut, cowpea, finger millet, pigeon pea, sorghum, vetch. Farmers in Africa and South America have introduced the world to a whole new alphabet of delicious, nutritious, heat-resistant crops.

FARM TO FORK
In 2070, we really understand where our food comes from. Food education in schools, vertical farms on our doorsteps and farm visits – all mean growing food is part of daily life.

9

SPACE
OUT OF THIS WORLD

As long as humans have existed, we have looked up at the night sky in wonder. How did we get here? Where are we going? Is there anyone else out there? In the coming decades, we will push towards answers to some of our deepest questions. Discoveries from space exploration will help life on Earth. New ways of seeing the cosmos will reignite our sense of wonder about the miracle of life. And our adventures trying to live on other planets will make us realise that Earth really is the best place in the universe for us to live.

For my birthday I took my friends to Out of this World, the new Space Centre. It was incredible. One of the main attractions is the ZeroG lab where you float!

It was the best fun ever - like jumping on a trampoline but never coming down.

Last year was the 100th anniversary of the first-ever Moon landing. So there was this huge moon exhibition and some amazing ancient footage from 1969. I was over the Moon (ha ha!) because my favourite astronaut Valentina Terry was doing a live feed from the lunar base.

We could join in virtually to walk on the surface of the Moon with her and even ride in her moon buggy!

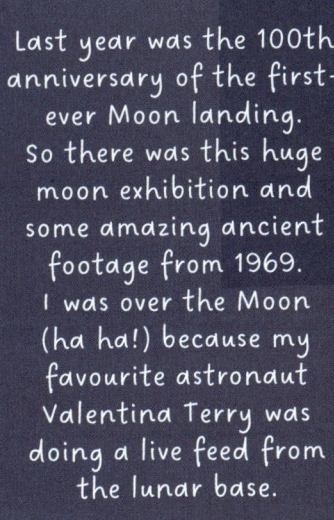

The ET zone was Jonah's favourite. They were showing one of the tardigrades they recently discovered on Jupiter's moon, Europa. We could look at it super huge in the quantum microscope. Even though it was just a cute little bug, it was the first time astrobiologists had found real living life outside of Earth. It got everyone thinking what else might be out there...

So we decided to welcome some aliens! The Stephen Hawking Probe sends messages into deep space, to places light years away. We queued up to send ours. We were allowed ten words each. Mine were 'Come to Earth! We have oxygen, water, gravity and friendship!'

FLY ME TO THE MOON – AND BEYOND!

Through the 21st century, humans ventured deeper into our solar system. At first, not everyone was convinced that space exploration was a priority. It seemed we had enough to fix on Earth. We needed to make sure that everyone on Earth would benefit from our explorations outside it. Planets and stars, like the oceans and the sky, are things we all share. By 2070, space exploration was for the good of all. This reawakened our ambition and sense of wonder, and our courage to venture into new worlds.

2037
International Moon Base build begins.

2036
Outer Space Treaty allows asteroid mining only 'for fairly shared human benefit.'

2034
Deep Space Endurance: astronauts circle the Moon for a year.

2033
Mars lander launched to return samples to Earth.

2027
James Webb space telescope reveals Big Bang's first galaxies.

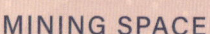

MINING SPACE
Some materials we need on Earth are really scarce here, but really common in asteroids and other planets. These include rare earth metals (clue's in the name) and even elements like helium-3 on the Moon, which could help breakthroughs in nuclear fusion.

REUSABLE ROCKETS
It seems crazy to spend billions on super-advanced technology that blows up! Developments in new materials allowed the creation of a new breed of reusable rocket. Space was opened up to new explorers as rockets became miles cheaper.

WHAT HAS SPACE EVER DONE FOR ME?
Exploring space has helped Earth in so many ways: robots, GPS, water purification, the cameras on our phones. In the future, space inventions might speed energy breakthroughs in solar or other technology that could help us have cheaper power on Earth.

Home 1.5 km

2069
'We are not alone' celebrations around the world on Moon landing centenary.

2067
Life found on Jupiter's moon, Europa.

2065
Crew arrives one year and 725 million kilometres later.

2064
Crew lifts off for first human mission to Jupiter.

2062
Mars celebrates its first city with stellar pageant.

2042
First liveable structures built on Mars remotely using 3D printers.

2043
Venus space station orbits the planets and prepares for slingshot to Mars.

2044
First human footsteps on the surface of Mars taken by Valentina Terry.

2045
Life on Mars! Evidence of fossil life found.

THE GREAT SPACE JUNK CLEAN UP
The first fine for space littering was in the 2020s. Since then, there's been a tonne of brilliant inventions for galactic garbage gobbling, as the number of satellites climbed to a mind-boggling half a million. Now they must all be reused or recycled.

LIFE ON MARS
Mars is around 225 million km away. You don't want to forget your toothbrush!

LUNAR BASE
Before you go camping in the wild, you'll probably try a couple of nights in your back garden. The Moon base was like that. It was a safe place to figure things out: how to make water to drink, oxygen to breathe, hydrogen for fuel. It made us ready for Mars and beyond.

2047
International 'Earth first' ruling says money made from space must help countries most affected by climate change.

2054
Habitable Worlds Observatory telescope sent to explore exoplanets.

2058
Mission to Saturn's rings 'live' beams images to everyone's smart phones.

2060
Solar eclipse across Africa coincides with first African nation winning the Olympics.

10

DEMOCRACY
POWER TO THE PEOPLE

The word democracy means 'rule by the people'. The idea is for everyone to have a say in decisions that affect them. For a long time, democracy didn't seem like that. People felt that just a few powerful people seemed to decide everything. By 2070, with the help of technology (giving good information), and thousands of new local ways to take part in decisions (giving us practice in arguing and finding agreement), society could, for the first time, live the dream of true democracy. Now it's something we are all a part of.

Today I dropped Mum off at the 'Big Think' (they used to be called 'Deliberative Assemblies' but when children got involved, they ditched that!). There's been a tonne of interest in this one. It's about whether we should let a robot become a Member of Parliament.

Big Thinks are a bit like juries (normal people have been deciding trials for thousands of years). Regular people (like Mum!) get picked at random to take part.

They listen to loads of evidence about the topic from all sides – from experts and from all the 'Little Thinkers' – which includes anyone who wants to give their views (Grammy and I went to the local 'view booth' to give ours).

AI helps manage all the information coming in and a (human) 'togetherer' helps keep the discussion on track.

Big Thinks involve a lot of talking. If you're a quiet person you can talk in writing or via other people – and it's important as quiet people often have the best ideas.

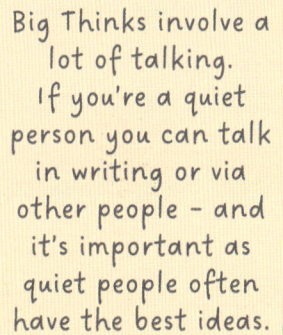 

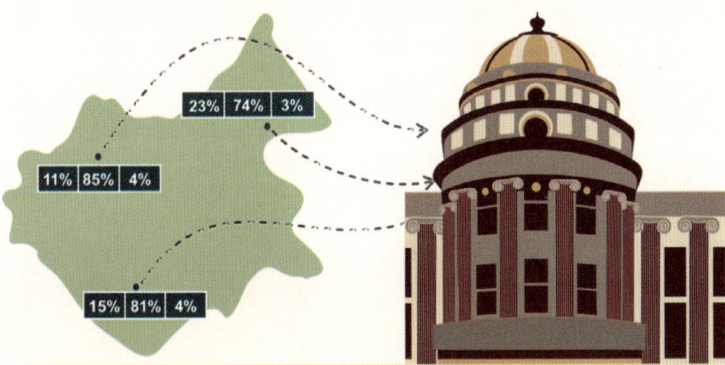

What the people decide will get put with all the other Big Think results around the country. We all have our say and politicians have to listen.

I'm not sure what I think about the robot MP yet, but Rafiki is dead against it. He says robots lack 'emotional intelligence'. Hmm, pretty emotionally intelligent comment, I reckon.

EVERY PERSON COUNTS

Change isn't easy. It usually starts small. Let's say you want to fix loneliness. You can start by chatting to someone who looks lonely in the playground. That's a brilliant start! To go further, you might need help. You could involve friends and family and take care of your street. You might involve your school to help your whole neighbourhood. You might talk to your local council or other organisations working on loneliness to help the whole city or even the country. Pretty soon you have a team, who all want change. Now we're talking! History has shown that a team of normal people caring enough to work together is a great way to change the world.

2027
The Wellbeing of Future Generations Act (UK) ensures governments consider long-term impact of policies.

2049
European Union makes 'National Wellbeing' its key measure.

2044
UK introduces a third house in the Houses of Parliament – The People's Palace.

WE ARE NOT ALONE
We all belong in communities. Being an active part of a community means caring about what happens in it, speaking up if things aren't right and respecting and listening to other people.

WHO COUNTS
Who counts when it comes to having a say? For centuries the answer was 'just a privileged few' but thankfully we evolved. We started by adding all the people. Then animals and plants, rivers and forests. Even robots and asteroids made the list. The more we added, the better we felt about the decisions we made.

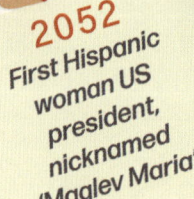

2052
First Hispanic woman US president, nicknamed 'Maglev Maria'.

2054
Protection of nature must now be considered in all political decisions.

2063
Trust in politics at highest level this century.

2028
First international citizen's assembly on AI rules.

2030
Citizen science project leads to Alzheimer's breakthrough.

2031
Whole of UK lowers voting age to 16.

2033
The end of fake news – AI turns out to be great at spotting fakes.

THE IMAGINARIUM
People got out of the habit of thinking positively about the future. They had good ideas but thought politicians wouldn't allow them. Now the People's Palace has 'The Imaginarium' where people use augmented reality to see their visions. Suddenly it seems there's nothing in the way of making them real.

2041
Manchester UK's 'rule by the people' involves public in every decision.

2039
New social media tool promotes areas of consensus instead of disagreement.

2035
Middle East 'Forgiveness Choir' win Nobel Peace Prize.

BAD NEWS
The news in the old days was often bad. It made us feel sad, helpless, pessimistic – and wrong. We thought the world couldn't be improved. But when we started using good data to tell different stories, we saw that tonnes had already got better. Knowing that made everyone excited about how much more we could do.

2065
'Young people's act' requires all companies world-wide to take future generations into consideration.

2068
Era of political parties is over as all MPs are independent.

2070
Royal Family agree to live on Universal Basic Income as an experiment.

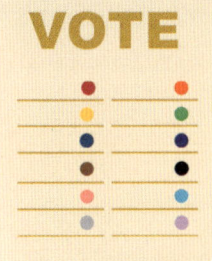

VOTE

THE JOURNEY STARTS HERE
ONE SMALL STEP

So what do you think? How do you feel about 2070? Are there things you're excited about? Things you'd like to be different? More greenery? More tech? More 3D-printed chocolate?

When we take time to look at the future, it can change how we see the present. We see that things we thought had to be a certain way could, with a big push, change. Things that are ok could be even better.

We wrote this book because optimism sometimes seems hard to come by. Even though people mostly feel quite optimistic about their own lives, they're often pessimistic about the world.

They think it's a bit stuck. But, in fact, in the last few decades we've made some of the biggest improvements to global health and poverty in human history. By understanding how much things have already changed, we can continue to improve things. And optimism is contagious!

We are especially keen on a particular kind of 'realistic optimism'. It's about more than just being hopeful; it's optimism based on facts and science and real possibilities.

Being a realistic optimist is also about what you do as much as how you think: finding and sharing good news with other people or taking time to notice the tiny things that remind us of the wonder of life. It's about looking for things that we like about other people instead of things we disagree with, and standing up against things that are wrong.

As we grow and become wiser as a society, we think more about what it means to live a good human life. Artificial intelligence has made us think even harder about what makes humans unique. And it's not just about being clever and knowing more (though learning is great). It's also about living, experiencing, seeing, hearing, moving, helping, creating, breathing, caring, dancing, playing, loving and imagining.

There is so much we can do with all that wonderful humanity! We can use it to create a really brilliant world.

And we all have a part to play. Working out what we want is an important first step. You need to have an idea of what you're building before you start hammering the nails.

So what is the world you want to live in? What's your future vision?

ABOUT THE AUTHORS

Madeleine Rogers' background is in illustration, graphic and product design. Recently graduated with an MA in Sustainable Design, her practice is focused on communicating wonder for the natural world to young audiences. She has authored and illustrated a series of books celebrating wildlife which have been translated into several languages.

Cathy Rogers is a science writer and researcher. Her career began in TV, creating and producing science programmes, including the Emmy-nominated Junkyard Wars(US) /Scrapheap Challenge (UK). Following a PhD in Educational Neuroscience, exploring how creativity works in the brain, she has written a book for teachers about how brains work. She speaks and writes on a range of subjects.

ACKNOWLEDGEMENTS

We are incredibly grateful to all the scientists who gave their time, expertise and enthusiasm to this project. We are also indebted to a host of friends and advisors who have helped us in myriad ways. We would like to thank Jonathan, Susie, Hanri, Robin and the team at GMC for their guidance and belief in this project. And our greatest thanks to our families for their encouragement, support and strong opinions.

First published 2024 by Button Books, an imprint of Guild of Master Craftsman Publications Ltd, Castle Place, 166 High Street, Lewes, East Sussex, BN7 1XU, UK. Text © Cathy Rogers, 2024. Illustrations © Madeleine Rogers, 2024. Copyright in the Work © GMC Publications Ltd, 2024. ISBN 978 1 78708 150 5. Distributed by Publishers Group West in the United States. All rights reserved. The right of Cathy Rogers to be identified as the author of this work has been asserted in accordance with the Copyright, Designs and Patents Act 1988, sections 77 and 78. No part of this publication may be reproduced, stored in a retrieval system, or transmitted in any form or by any means without the prior permission of the publisher and copyright owner. Views and comments expressed by the author do not necessarily represent those of the publishers. The publishers and author can accept no legal responsibility for any consequences arising from the application of information, advice, or instructions given in this publication. A catalogue record for this book is available from the British Library. Publisher: Jonathan Bailey, Production: Jim Bulley, Senior Project Editor: Susie Behar, Designer: Hanri van Wyk, Additional design: Emily Hurlock, Illustrator: Madeleine Rogers. Colour origination by GMC Reprographics. Printed and bound in China.

For more on Button Books, contact:

GMC Publications Ltd, Castle Place,
166 High Street, Lewes, East Sussex,
BN7 1XU, United Kingdom
Tel: +44 (0)1273 488005
buttonbooks.co.uk/buttonbooks.us